ALL ABOUT SPIDERS

Written By: Anna DiGilio

All rights reserved. No part of this publication may be reproduced, distributed, or transmitted in any form or by any means, including photocopying, recording, or other electronic or mechanical methods, without the prior written permission of the publisher, except in the case of brief quotations embodied in critical reviews and certain other noncommercial uses permitted by copyright law.

For permission requests, write to the publisher:
Laprea Publishing
info@lapreapublishing.com

Website: www.GuidedReaders.com

ISBN: 978-1-64579-009-9

© 2017 Anna DiGilio
www.SimplySkilledTeaching.com

Printed in the United States of America

TABLE OF CONTENTS

Arachnids not Insects .... Page 4

Spider Shapes and Sizes .... Page 5

The Body of a Spider .... Page 6

The Spinnerets .... Page 7

The Spider's Habitat .... Page 8

Why Do Spiders Make Webs? .... Page 9

Harmful Spiders .... Page 10

Spiders Help the Environment .... Page 11

Spiders Help Mankind .... Page 12

Glossary .... Page 13

Arachnids not Insects

Spiders are not insects. They are called <u>arachnids</u>. Spiders have eight legs. Insects have six legs. Insects have feelers called <u>antennae</u> on their heads. Spiders do not. Insects have three body parts. Spiders have two.

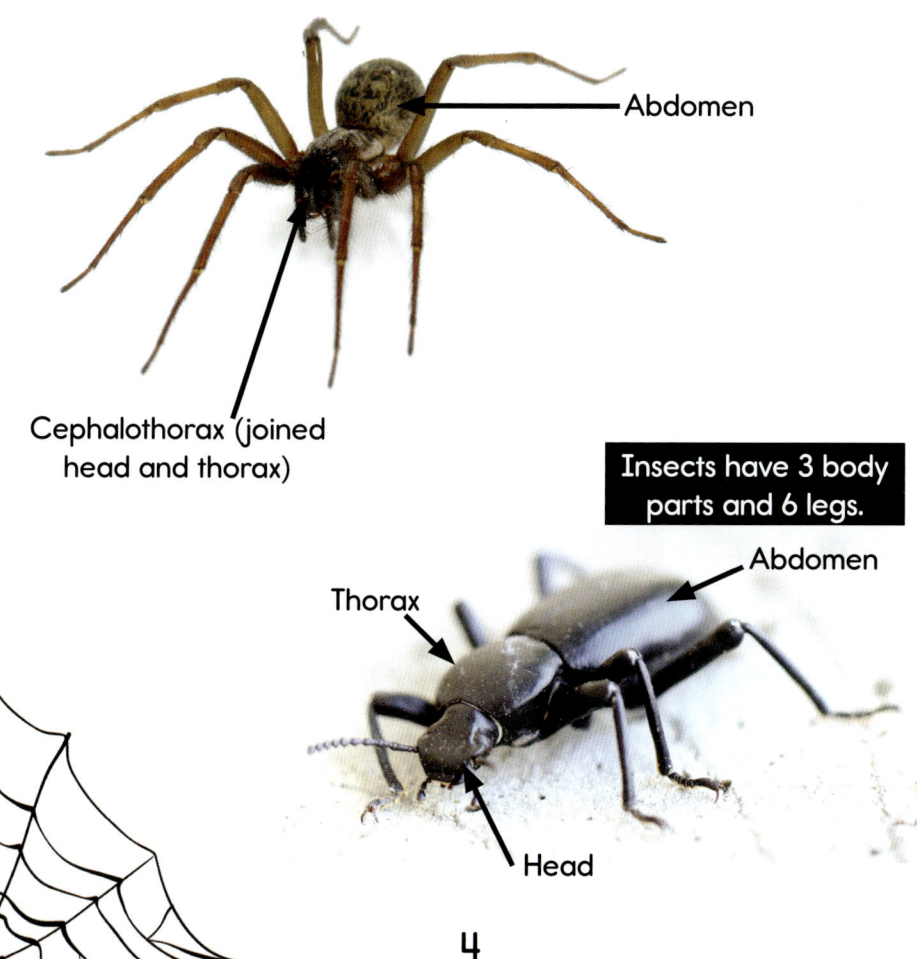

Spiders have 2 body parts and 8 legs.

Abdomen

Cephalothorax (joined head and thorax)

Insects have 3 body parts and 6 legs.

Abdomen

Thorax

Head

Spider Shapes and Sizes

Spiders have the same shape. They come in many sizes. Some are tiny. Some are big.

Spiders are many colors. They are brown. They are black. They are yellow, green, gray, and red. Some spiders can even change color!

The Body of a Spider

A spider has two body parts. One is the <u>cephalothorax</u>. The spider's eyes and mouth are on the front of the cephalothorax. The legs are also on this part. There are four legs on each side. The other body part is the abdomen.

The Spinnerets

Spiders have <u>spinnerets</u>. They are in the abdomen. Spinnerets make thread. Spiders use it to make webs.

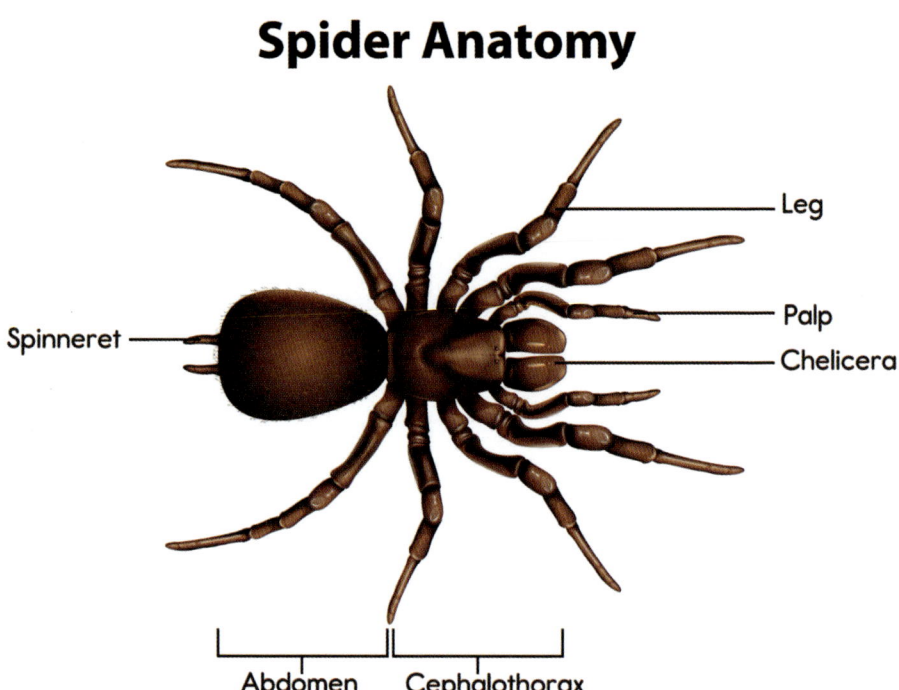

The Spider's Habitat

Spiders live almost everywhere. But they do not live at the South Pole. They do not live in the ocean. They usually do not live on high mountains. Spiders like the dark. They make their homes there. Spiders live in basements. Spiders live in dead logs. Think of other places you may find spiders.

Why Do Spiders Make Webs?
Spider webs are sticky. Spiders spin webs to trap insects. Insects stick to the web. Spiders bite them with their fangs. Insects are spider food.

Harmful Spiders

Most spiders are not harmful. But some spiders are harmful. One is the black widow. Another is the tarantula. Black widow spiders live everywhere. Tarantulas mainly live in deserts, rain forests, and jungles.

Black widow

Tarantula

Spiders Help the Environment

Spiders help the environment. They eat many insects. Then there are less bugs on the planet. Insects can be harmful. They could destroy crops. They could destroy <u>ecosystems</u>!

Spiders are also part of the <u>food chain</u>. They are food for birds and other animals.

This spider is eating an ant.

Spiders Help Mankind

Spiders help mankind. Scientists study their <u>venom</u>. Scientists study spider webs. They use them as a model to make things. Spiders are very interesting creatures!

GLOSSARY

<u>antennae</u>
thin, sensitive organs on the head of an insect used mainly to feel and touch things

<u>arachnids</u>
animals that have eight legs and bodies formed of two parts

<u>cephalothorax</u>
the joined head and thorax of spiders

<u>ecosystems</u>
everything that exists in certain environments, including living things and non-living things

GLOSSARY

<u>food chain</u>
how each living thing gets food and how nutrients are passed from creature to creature

<u>spinnerets</u>
organs through which the silk or thread of spiders is produced

<u>venom</u>
a poison that is produced by an animal and used to kill or injure another animal, usually through biting or stinging